A special gift for:

_____

From:

_____

Date:

_____

When You
Haven't
Got A
Prayer

*Answers
You Want...
Answers
You Get!*

KAREN MOORE

To my sister, Donna,
who is always a loving answer
to my prayers.

Dear Father in Heaven,
Thank You for Your love and mercy.
Thank You for watching over my life.
Lord, I've lost my way
and I'm trying to hold on
and believe You hear me
and that You will help me
move forward again.
I confess that I feel weak
and I come to You now for strength
and direction.
In Jesus' name I pray.
AMEN.

(A Prayer for Strength from Karen)

Introduction

BOOKS THAT GUIDE US through the prayer process are wonderful and we're blessed with abundant resources. The intention of this book, however, is to encourage beginners and prayer warriors alike when you reach the point of prayer exhaustion. At one time or another, we've all reached the place of frustration, or apathy, or uncertainty about prayer. Sometimes we might feel as if we've prayed all we can about something, and we just don't have it in us to keep going. We don't know what else to say, we've run out of steam about the issue, or we're not even sure any more if answers will ever come.

But when we offer prayers for someone else, or for something incredibly important in our own lives, we begin with the hopeful feeling that God is there for us and is listening. We believe God will answer, and we pray with intense heart and mind and soul.

When You Haven't Got a Prayer can help you keep believing that a loving Heavenly Father hears you and walks with you and will never leave you without an answer. When at first you don't succeed, pray, pray again!

Blessings to You,
Karen

Introduced to Prayer

MY FIRST REAL MEMORY OF PRAYER came with an instant answer. I was probably six or seven years old and I recall a sense of frustration about not knowing if I did the whole prayer thing "right." Looking back, I'm not even sure how I knew prayer was important, but somehow I did. We were sort of random church-goers then, though my mom was an avid Bible reader. I knew prayer went on in church or when we had dinner at our great-grandma's house, but I can't say I had any real understanding of what it was all about. I was curious.

Somehow, in our old house situated all alone on a dirt road, adjacent to over grown woods where we could play and climb trees, God figured out where I lived and answered a prayer. I simply asked the "how" of prayer one morning and the answer came the very next day.

Two young evangelists *happened by* and knocked on our door. They had to be pretty off the beaten track to be on our little old dirt road with only four houses in about a two mile stretch. Mom just loved sharing her Bible readings with random preachers so it wasn't unusual that she was standing in the doorway having a conversation with them when I walked by. I suspect she also just enjoyed seeing another adult in the neighborhood, since she was a young woman with four active little girls. Anyway, it was at one of those moments when I heard one door-to-door preacher ask, "Do you know the four steps of how to pray?"

Well, I nearly fell over! I don't know what mom answered or if she knew the steps, but I was instantly stopped in my tracks, ready to get the answer to my very own prayer. I had just asked God the question and here was the answer. Incidentally, I've been using a version of those four steps ever since that day and you'll see my version of that later in this book.

After that experience, I thought the whole thing was pretty simple. I couldn't believe how easy it all was! You have a concern or something on your heart and you take it to God. He tells you what the answer is, and just like magic, everything is happy again!

Well, I felt pretty fine about that until somewhere around the age of ten when a whole different event made the prayer walls come tumbling down.

It started with a phone call from my uncle to my parents. My uncle was a volunteer fireman, and a young couple that my parents knew had just perished in a fire in their home. The couple had a young baby and since their home was insulated with asbestos, the fire couldn't get out and the heat became incredible. They wrapped their young baby in a big blanket and threw her out the second story window in an effort to save her life. Thankfully, she survived, though she had many operations for skin burns.

Everything in that house burned except one thing—their family Bible. Wasn't it made of paper? Hearing this story and seeing my parents' unhappiness, I was sure that if I just prayed hard enough, God could fix this and make everything okay again. I prayed and cried for nearly two weeks, or so it seemed. Finally, I realized that God wasn't going to "fix" this. He didn't bring the young couple back, or keep that poor burned baby from years of pain and anguish. It was my first reality check about prayer.

At six, I thought it was all simple. At ten, I discovered it was not. Today, I don't want to suggest that I've gotten all the answers about how or why it works, or if there are any magic formulas. But I do want to suggest that it works…and it works every time!

It works every time because it doesn't depend on how smart we are, or how much faith we have, or whether we sat in the right position, said the right words using the best grammar ever, or clasped our hands or raised them…it works because every time we whisper, shout, or speak God's name with a heart toward Him, we're connected to His answering service and He always gets the message.

If it feels like you're only getting a busy signal, or you've been on hold for a very long time…read on and we'll try to reconnect you. The good news is that Jesus paid the bill in full so that you can call anytime at all, and your Father will answer.

Reading about the answered prayers of others can renew our spirits. It reminds us that we are not alone in our journey. It is my hope that this book gives you the encouragement, the desire, and the heart to try prayer one more time.

You may feel like you haven't got a prayer…but God wants you to know that you always do. Whatever your need, whatever your hope, whatever you're going through today, take my hand…we're in it together and our God is already just ahead of us.

So Is Anybody Really Listening?

ONCE UPON A TIME, there was a farmer who had a great field and after preparing the soil, he planted it with beautiful vegetables that would sustain him for the winter. Once the field was fully planted, he thanked the Lord and asked Him to watch over it, bless it, and let it grow to harvest. Within days of his prayer, the field sprouted a covering of seedlings and things were well underway.

It wasn't long after his prayer, however, that the farmer began to worry about drought and pestilence and other things that could ruin his crops. He worried so much that the land dried up and the rodents began to eat the young plants that had begun to bloom. Before long, the field was nearly in ruins and the man prayed again, "Lord, why did You let my beautiful field go to waste? Why didn't You protect it and help it grow?"

The Lord answered, "When you first planted the field, I blessed it. You asked me to watch over it and I did and it grew. Then you started to watch over it. You worried about floods and drought and pests. You took over the watching, so I stepped back. I've given you the place to plant, the tender seeds to nourish, but the rain and the sun are mine. You began by putting the field in my care, but then you took it back to care for it on your own. Would you rather keep going on your own, or would you like me to come back in and take over watching the field?"

The man bowed his head. "Lord, please watch over me and my thoughts and fears, watch over my fields and the harvest, and then we will all surely grow."

The Lord answered, "And so it shall be!"

Sometimes when we think God isn't answering or when we think He's not listening, we should stop and see if we've gotten in the way of His plans for us. Mother Teresa was often quoted as saying, "Just let me get out of the way," in order to get God's work done. Sometimes, that needs to be our prayer.

Lord,

When I get in Your way,

remind me that YOU KNOW

what You're doing. Remind me to leave

the fields of doubt and self-pity,

and grumbling behind, so that there's room

for You to plant MERCY,

and PEACE, and GRACE in my heart.

AMEN

Be humble under God's powerful hand
so he will lift you up when the right time comes.
Give all your worries to him,
because he cares about you.

1 PETER 5:6-7 NCV

Do Miracles Still Happen?

DO YOU EVER WONDER if God still performs miracles? Well, I'm here to say that He does, and what better way to understand that than in a two-part prayer story...one about a baby, and one about love.

Part One: The Baby Story

My friend, Collette, is a vibrant, warm and loving person. She is a school teacher, happily married and a total delight to be around. As we became closer friends, she confided to me that she and her husband were very much hoping to have a baby, but after going through all kinds of tests, it looked like that wasn't meant to be. After trying different therapies and treatments, they were finally told to join a support group for couples who want babies, but can't have them. The facts were that her husband had zero sperm count and she had some extreme cervical issues.

One day, after another session at the clinic, Collette stopped by my house and we talked about the whole thing one more time. I told Collette that if anyone deserved to have a baby it was her, and that I did not believe God intended for her to go childless. From that point on, I was determined to make this a prayer mission.

Sometimes it's great to have a mission for someone else, because it reminds you about how the system works and brings you back to more fervent prayers for things in your own life. You can always find a way to have a prayer mission.

At that time, my sister, Donna, and I were in the habit of taking three-mile walks around the streets where we lived and we'd use those occasions to discuss life and love and the needs of others. Donna was one of my prayer partners and she knew Collette as well, so I suggested we make it a special mission to pray for Collette and her husband and their desire for a baby. We also decided to pray a date, something neither of us had ever done before, to see if God would honor the prayer if we were more specific. I know opinions on these things differ in theological circles, but we weren't trying to be theologians, we just wanted to focus our prayers. We agreed to pray that Collette would be pregnant by Mother's Day. It was mid-January when we started.

As the weeks and months passed, I was continually in communication with Collette and discovered that after going to four different teams of doctors, trying very expensive fertilization programs, and everything anyone could imagine, they finally joined that support group. Time and time again, we would share tears of sadness, but something in me wouldn't give up on the idea that this was not going to be the outcome. As winter turned to spring and March to April, there was still no obvious change and Collette and her husband began to try harder to accept the situation. Maybe they could, but I couldn't.

A few days before Mother's Day, Collette and I talked again, and I realized to my dismay that the doctors were not changing their view. A pregnancy would take a miracle, and that's all there was to it. At least I knew we had put the problem in the right hands. When Mother's Day came, Collette called me to wish me a happy Mother's Day, and choking back my tears and not knowing what else to say, I thanked her. As we were easing by the topic, she suddenly yelled into the phone, "Karen, I think I'm pregnant!" Well, that was a show stopper! The tears began falling down my cheeks in a new way.

"What makes you think so?" I asked. "Did you do a test?"

"Two!" came the triumphant word. "They both came out positive!"

She had already made an appointment to see her doctor who probably was quite sure that it was just wishful thinking on her part. Later, her doctor admitted that there was no explanation, beyond some kind of miracle. I was overcome with awe and amazement for the loving God who had answered this prayer so wonderfully.

When my sister came to walk with me that evening, I waited a bit before telling her the news. I wanted it to be just the right moment. Finally, I couldn't stand it any longer and burst out with the whole story. We must have looked like two crazy women as we were out there on the sidewalk jumping up and down and crying. We were so excited! As we settled down and walked and talked some more, we started thinking about another unanswered prayer and thought maybe it was time to get more serious about that one as well. After all, we were on a roll.

Part Two: The Love Story

While the doctor was still shaking her head in disbe-lief, and Collette was busy preparing a nursery, she and her husband decided it would be good to have some electrical work done in their basement. After all, they'd have to put her husband's study downstairs now to make room for the baby upstairs. This turned out to be a most God-inspired decision.

The fourth of July happens to be my birthday, and the now happily pregnant Collette called me to wish me a happy birthday. Just the sound of her voice made me happy and I thanked God every time I thought of her. After we discussed my impending birthday plans, she said the funniest thing. "Karen, there's a really nice guy working in my basement on all that electrical stuff, and for some reason, whenever I see him, I get a picture of your sister, Donna."

Now Collette did not know about the Mother's Day walk when Donna and I had agreed to pray specifically one more time for her to meet her life partner. We had agreed that Donna would at least meet the man she would marry by the first of August. Well, I have to say, that God never seems to answer these prayers a moment too soon, and when Collette made that comment, I was all over it.

"Collette, you get off the phone and go down to your basement and find out if this nice guy is single," I laughed. She hesitated for a moment.

"What will he think of my asking such a question when I'm three months pregnant and my husband isn't home?" She asked.

"I don't care," was all I could get out. "Go and ask him and see if he's willing to meet a really wonderful woman and then call me back."

A few minutes later, a laughing Collette called me again. "He's single!" she shouted. She told me that he had been single now for five years and he seemed to be a quiet kind of guy, but he reluctantly took the phone number for my sister. It was already the first week of July.

As it turned out, he was shy and it took another two weeks before he mustered up the courage to actually call Donna. In fact, through a lot of pleading on my part to get her to call him, she finally left a one sentence timid line on his answering machine about hoping to hear from him soon.

Two more days passed, but by the third week of July, he called and they talked for several hours on the phone and then made plans to meet on the 25th. (I later learned that Collette had transposed two of the numbers so Bill did not have the right number until the timid phone call that Donna made—another little aspect of the grace of God.) They met at a restaurant for lunch, talked until dinner time and made plans to meet the following week. It was love! Okay, they dated, got to know each other, then it was love. But it happened and they just celebrated their tenth anniversary!

I can't say I've done that kind of praying as much since, but something in me knows that both of those miracles are a direct result of the faith behind those prayers and a benevolent God who chose to answer them so beautifully. A wonderful baby boy and a warm and loving husband could only come from His hand.

Lord,

You are so awesome

and it is truly incredible

to our HEARTS AND MINDS

the things that prayer

can accomplish.

Thank You for being

a God of *miracles*.

Thank You

for *loving* us so much.

AMEN

In a universe beyond our comprehension

we open our hearts and minds

to what we call the Creator and Sustainer of all,

hoping against hope that we shall find guidance

in our search for a life of value.

Brief as we know it to be, we want that life

to have meaning, to be defined by virtue,

and to have been—in the final analysis—worth living.

Whatever means we use to fulfill our yearning,

it will be a form of prayer, voiced or not.

ALAN C. MERMANN

God's Answers Are Always Creative!

WHEN WE GO THROUGH major disappointment time and again, it can get harder to keep praying. It's at that point we should acknowledge that God's plan and His answer don't always come in a form that we expect, but may be even bigger than what we had in mind. Read "Baby, Baby" and you'll see what I mean.

Baby, Baby

After two miscarriages, Kelly decided to make an appointment with a reproductive specialist. She and her husband had prayed and prayed for a baby, but Kelly finally started to think it just wasn't in God's plan. Her husband, on the other hand, wasn't willing to give up. He kept on believing. Perhaps for a bit, he even believed for both of them.

After seeing the specialist, Kelly found out that she had a genetic blood-clotting disorder that was causing her to miscarry. She would be allowed to take certain blood thinners to help her go to full term once she was pregnant again. What a relief! Just knowing there was an answer to the problem helped Kelly and her husband begin to hope again, and that in itself was an answer to their prayers.

Following the consultation with a specialist, the couple tried again and Kelly was pregnant within two months. Two months into that pregnancy, the ultrasound showed that everything looked good, and Kelly believed the blood thinners were doing the job to keep the baby growing inside of her.

But, it was not to be. Before the third month, this pregnancy was also lost. All the hopes and dreams and prayers for a baby were gone again. Kelly felt betrayed and heartbroken. How could God do this? She had been faithful in prayer. She had trusted and loved Him for so long. Her mind raced to the millions of teens having unwanted babies and the millions of babies who were abused and neglected. Why? All she wanted was to love her own wonderful baby. Why didn't God answer her prayer? Why didn't He save this tiny life she already cherished? She wasn't sure she cared now about the answer. She was angry and out of prayers. Prayer didn't work. She was out of hope.

Hope is the candle we keep in the window
of our hearts to keep us clear about the path before
us and the steps to take. Sometimes that hope
seems to be snuffed out, and for a moment we are
left in the darkness, separated from the light,
the thing we so desperately need.

But as Albert Schweitzer reminds us,
"Sometimes our light goes out,
but is blown into flame by another human being.
Each of us owes deepest thanks
to those who have rekindled this light."

Kelly's light was out...or so she thought. Little did she know just then that her hope was about to be rekindled. In the meantime, she and her husband were determined to adjust to the circumstances that had been thrust upon them. They considered adoption, but were undecided. Her husband continued to pray for them both.

During a family gathering a short time later, Kelly and her sister-in-law began talking about the miscarriages. A woman of great heart with three children of her own, her sister-in-law offered an option that would be just the light Kelly needed to bring a new flame to her candle of hope. "I'll carry a baby for you," she said.

Kelly was awed by the offer and she and her husband prayed long and hard over this opportunity. Her sister-in-law explained that she wanted Kelly and her brother to know what it was like to hug and kiss and be blessed by a child of their own and that she would be glad to be a surrogate mother.

After weeks of prayers, legal documentation, medical tests, and special medications, they were ready to begin the process. By now, Kelly had two embryos growing in her uterus and they would be transferred into her sister-in-law's womb. Within ten days, they'd know if pregnancy had happened or not. They had no choice but to wait and pray.

The Bible talks a lot about waiting on the Lord. Most of us find this extremely hard to do. We might declare with the Psalmist, *"Lord, why are you so far away? Why do you hide when there is trouble?"* (NCV) Yet, we wait because we can do no other.

When the waiting was over, Kelly and her husband learned that the procedure was indeed successful. They were shocked, thrilled, and ecstatic! Yet, the bitter experiences from before left Kelly with a fear she couldn't quite shake. She decided she would not get too excited until the pregnancy was at least halfway along.

When her sister-in-law started to experience bleeding, Kelly was sure that God was taking this baby away as well. She and her husband discussed the possibility of yet another loss and drew some new conclusions. If this baby was lost, they would not try again. It was too much of an emotional rollercoaster and neither of them wanted to ride any further. They were worn out spiritually and emotionally.

When a new ultrasound was conducted, the doctor could see only one gestational sac and though that was disappointing, it looked to be healthy and that was a relief. They all waited while the doctor kept quietly doing the ultrasound. Kelly was worried that the doctor was keeping something from them. The doctor finally smiled and said, "You're not going to believe this, but you have twins." Sure enough, in one gestational sac, two tiny circles. Circles of love!

As of today, the healthy twins have been born to Kelly and her husband, and they have been uplifted by this answered prayer. All that happened before serves to remind them that God is faithful and continues in the effort to bless His children. For Kelly, this experience brings new life to her understanding of prayer as well.

The image that best expresses
the intimacy we share with God during prayer
is the image of God's breath.
We receive a new breath, a new freedom,
and a new life. This new life
is the divine life of God Himself.
Prayer, therefore, is God's breathing into us,
which allows us to become part of
the intimacy of God's inner life
and be born anew.

HENRI NOUWEN

Knocking On the Door of Despair

MOTHERS HAVE ALWAYS HAD a special relationship with their children and sometimes that is especially so for mothers and sons. Mothers who pray for their children provide a banner of love like no other. It's certain that Rolf will never forget the special answer to prayer he and his mother received.

As a young man of 22, Rolf was a single missionary serving in Puerto Rico and selling Christian books door-to-door. For two and a half years, he walked around visiting some 70,000 homes and leading many people to the Lord. It was challenging and rewarding work and he sold thousands of books.

Early on in this experience, Rolf's brother came to visit and spent a month with him. They decided to take two weeks to sell books and talk with people and then two weeks to share island adventures and have fun. It was a wonderful time for them both.

When the day came for his brother to leave, a crushing heaviness settled in on Rolf. He realized how lonely he felt and became discouraged. He couldn't even work up a goodbye smile.

After his brother was gone, Rolf went back on the road, but on the first day back, he didn't sell a single book and contemplated going back to the States. Suddenly the island adventure didn't seem like so much fun anymore. As he sat in bumper-to-bumper traffic, slumped over the steering wheel in his old van, he was figuratively, emotionally, and literally unable to move. He sat in his depressed thoughts going nowhere.

But God was watching and somewhere out there, someone else held him up. Perhaps her prayers went something like this:

> *Lord, please remind Rolf that Your peace is within him today. Help him to trust that he is exactly where he is supposed to be. Help him delight in the beautiful possibilities before him and to try to hold on to the reasons he went to Puerto Rico to begin with. As he uses the gifts You have given him and passes on the love within his heart, please bless him. May Your presence, Lord, settle into his heart and mind and body, wherever he is today. May his soul awaken in joy, be uplifted in song, and praise You for all that is before him. Hold him up, Lord. Lift his troubled heart and mind and bring him peace. Amen.*

Whatever wonderful prayer Rolf's mother uttered to her Lord, it worked. All of a sudden, the heaviness lifted and the loneliness was swept away. It was real. He could feel it in his bones. For the first time since his brother left, Rolf sat up straight and smiled and thanked the Lord for taking his load. He looked at his watch to see what time it was as he felt so remarkably strong and happy. When he got home that day, he wrote his mother a note to tell her about the amazing experience. He told her exactly the time that it happened and he asked if she had been praying for him during that time.

When her letter arrived in the mail several days later, Rolf could barely put it down. His mother wrote that she had been carrying a burden for him for three days and though she didn't know what the problem was, she knew she needed to pray.

On the third day of continual prayer, Rolf's mother and her husband were driving to pick up his brother after his return from the trip to Puerto Rico. It was late June of 1966, and the car had no air conditioning. Unable to bear the burden for Rolf any longer, his mother turned her head toward the open window of the car and prayed "in the Spirit." She didn't remember how long she prayed that way, but when she finished, the heavy burden she had carried was gone. She felt it physically lift from her body and when she looked at her watch, she saw that it was 4:30. It was indeed the exact same time that Rolf felt his burden lift from the loneliness he was experiencing in that traffic jam in San Juan. As Rolf put down his mother's letter, he knew that God indeed was there with him. He knew that from that moment on, he would never be alone.

Neither Rolf nor his mother ever forgot that divine answer to prayer. His mother remained a dedicated prayer warrior until the day she went to be with her Lord at the beautiful age of 94.

We cannot find God in noise and agitation. Nature: trees, flowers, and grass grow in silence. The stars, the moon, and the sun move in silence. What is essential is not what we say but what God tells us and what He tells others through us.

In silence He listens to us;
in silence He speaks to our souls.
In silence we are granted
the privilege
of listening to His voice.

Silence of our eyes.
Silence of our ears.
Silence of our mouths.
Silence of our minds.
...in the silence of the heart
God will speak.

Mother Teresa

33

Prayer Warriors

A PRAYER WARRIOR is a person who is convinced that God is omnipotent—that God has the power to do anything, to change anyone, and to intervene in any circumstance. A person who truly believes this refuses to doubt God.

When that doubt has replaced your ability to pray, may you, too, be blessed with a prayer warrior to lift the burdens off of your heart and soul.

One of the most powerful kinds of prayers that any prayer warrior puts forth is one where no doubt is allowed to lurk anywhere. Jesus told His followers, "I tell you the truth, you can say to this mountain, 'Go, fall into the sea.' And if you have no doubts in your mind and believe that what you say will happen, God will do it for you. So I tell you to believe that you have received the things you ask for in prayer, and God will give them to you. " (Mark 11:23-24 NCV)

There's probably a reason why the office of prayer warrior is difficult to obtain. Most of us aren't very good at removing that tiny bit of doubt when we pray. Sometimes though, we're in a position where we're not willing to let doubt slip in. Sometimes we absolutely believe because we need an answer on the spot. A couple of short stories follow to illustrate the point.

Just a Little Rain

SOME YEARS AGO, a friend of mine was attending a small college in an upstate New York town. She lived over twenty miles from the school and had to travel a six lane highway to get back and forth from her home. One afternoon in late March, she was traveling in the fast lane, clicking off the miles to school. She had been forced to use her window washer fluid a number of times because the passing cars would splash muddy residue on her windshield from the morning rains. There was no snow left on the roadside. It was just a gray, muddy day.

About halfway to school, Cindy's car was hit by a big muddy mass from a passing truck. As Cindy went to wipe it off, the mud just smeared more, making it even harder to see out of the window. She tried the washer fluid, but it had gone dry and now she was going 70 miles an hour down a highway where she couldn't see a thing. In desperation, she cried out to the Lord. "Lord, please give me some rain on my window because I can't see a thing."

As she was attempting to slow her speed, and get the mud to clear, she realized that as she kept wiping, water did seem to be coming from somewhere onto the window pane. She kept wiping her window and gulped as she saw rain totally cleaning the pane. She was so grateful and for a moment, could hardly take in the fact that she was the only one she could see with her windshield wipers running. It didn't look like it was raining anywhere but on her car window.

As she drove to school, she thanked God over and over again for the rain. She could hardly believe it had happened, but she knew it had and whether anyone else would ever believe the story, she didn't care. She had called out to God in a moment of need, and He had answered. She was flooded with sunshine.

Whoever phrased the idea that "into each life a little rain must fall" might be surprised at the truth of it. In Cindy's case, that rain was a welcome sight.

Angel in a Tow Truck

IN MY MID-TWENTIES, I lived in Hicksville, Long Island. Hicksville is a booming city and like all the Island cities, one runs into the other with scarcely a sense of division.

At the time, I was attending a Bible study in a neighborhood many miles from where I lived and I wasn't terribly familiar with the side streets. One night, after a rather late study, I was heading home around 11:00 or so, when my engine overheated and my car broke down. I was going down a fairly dark side street at the time but managed to pull up under a street light and tried to assess the situation. This was before cell phones were part of daily life, so I used the only answering service I knew. I said a prayer. "Lord, I'm not sure where I am or just what to do right now. I do need help though, and I'm kind of afraid to get out of the car and go look for help at this late hour. Please send me some help. Amen."

My "Amen" was still pretty fresh on my lips, when a tow truck pulled up beside me. "Do you need some help, ma'am?" the guy asked politely.

"Well, it looks like I do," I said. "My husband will be getting worried about me soon."

I wouldn't do this today, but at the time, I was so convinced that this long-haired, big guy was some kind of angel, that when he suggested I get in his truck so he could take me home, get my husband, and come back to take care of the car, I did just that.

I don't remember his name, but I remember believing that God sent him to help me. He did just as he said he would. The truck driver took me home, picked up my husband, and they went back and took care of the car. It was a pretty awesome moment to me.

When I told my Bible study group the next week, they all agreed that the guy just may have been an angel. It always makes me think of the verse in Hebrews that suggests, "Don't forget to show hospitality to strangers, for some who have done this have entertained angels without realizing it." Whether he was a real angel, I'll never know, but that night, he was definitely an angel to me, sent by a loving Heavenly Father.

The Grateful Tread

THOSE MOTOR VEHICLE ANGELS are pretty wonderful and it seems that a lot of us have had the benefit of their silent help. When I think about how many near accidents I've missed, I have to give God the glory. I'm very sure that angels played a part in my well-being.

Years ago, a friend of mine remarked that every time she and her family would go anywhere in the car, she would say a prayer that went something like this: "Lord, please go before us to protect us today as we drive to our destination and stay behind us to keep us safe and let us not be the cause of any accident or injury, nor let anyone cause any harm to us as well. Amen."

Much of the time since then, her prayer has played in my mind and I often find myself repeating it without even realizing it. It's served me well more than once.

One of the most memorable times was while I was driving 75 miles an hour on the straight stretch from Colorado Springs to Denver with my business partner. We were just outside the Denver city limits in the fast lane, when Jeanne thought she heard a noise coming from the car.

I didn't hear anything at first, but then I saw smoke coming from the rear driver's side tire through the window. I tried to slow down as well as I could and find a place to get off the highway in a rather unforgiving expanse of cars. As the smoke poured forth into the air, I finally saw a place about one car space in width where I could pull over, though I was still on the fast lane side of the highway. When the car was stopped I said, "I guess we have a flat tire." Jeanne got out to take a closer look.

She came back and with a smile on her face, she said, "You don't have a flat tire, you have no tire!" While she was out looking at the tire, I started praying for help. I heard what she said, but it didn't really dawn on me until I got out of the car myself.

I stepped out to see that the tire was indeed not flat, it was totally blown apart! It's a wonder that we avoided a big accident on that high speed road. Just as I was looking at the tire, a big orange utility truck slowed down and angled itself behind my car in a very protective way.

Two burly guys got out and walked toward us. "Need a little help?" they called. To my amazement, they were there within minutes of the whole thing. They were shocked at how badly the tire was blown apart and how lucky we were to be safe.

After they changed the tire for us, we offered to pay them for their trouble, but they wouldn't take any money. They just wished us a good day and went back to their truck, waiting till we were safely on our way again to pull out. Jeanne and I were amazed. We were safe, we were grateful and there was no doubt that God had quickly answered a prayer.

faith

In Matthew 7:7, Jesus is quoted as saying, "Ask, and it will be given to you; seek, and you will find; knock, and it will be opened to you." (NKJV) We ask in faith, we seek in hope, and we knock because our Father has given us an open door.

hope

love

*Until now you have not asked for
anything in my name.
Ask and you will receive,
so that your joy will be the fullest possible joy.*

JOHN 16:24 NCV

*Jesus answered, "I tell you the truth,
if you have faith and do not doubt,
you will be able to do what I did
to this tree and even more.
You will be able to say to this mountain,
'Go, fall into the sea.'
And if you have faith, it will happen."*

MATTHEW 21:21 NCV

VERSES CAN COMFORT US and motivate us to keep trying and keep asking. Sometimes they can make us question our faith. Why aren't there more withered trees and mountains jumping up and throwing themselves into the sea? Is it truly because we don't have the faith it requires for Mother Nature to obey us? Perhaps, that's not what Jesus was after anyway. Perhaps those examples just serve the purpose of showing us that we can ask for anything if we ask in His name. His promise to us is that He is working with us to make us completely happy.

In God We Trust

TOM REMEMBERED an uncertain time in his life. He was down-sized from a job and working hard to find a new one. As the weeks turned into months, he wasn't feeling very certain that God was hearing his prayers. He and his wife continued to faithfully pray and believe as his severance dwindled away without a job in sight.

After months of searching for a new position, Tom was finally given a possibility of a good job at two different companies. One job was in Nashville and the other was in Grand Rapids. He and his wife wanted to go where they felt the Lord most wanted them to be. Since both jobs were similar in responsibility and pay, they prayed more and waited patiently for the Lord's answer. They agreed that they felt a desire in their hearts to go to Grand Rapids. It was a place where they felt at home and had friends and family.

Just as everything was looking good for the decision to move to Grand Rapids, Tom was informed that the parent company had just issued a big hiring freeze and they were no longer able to offer the position. The pressure to get a job was on as the severance pay disappeared from Tom's bank account. He could always accept the other job in Nashville, but by now, they were poised and ready to go to Grand Rapids. They needed God to intervene. They kept on praying.

Knowing he had to do something, Tom called the company in Grand Rapids and told them he wouldn't be able to wait for the freeze to lift because he needed a job and would have to take another offer. The company asked him to give them one more day. Tom waited and prayed.

The next morning, Tom got a call from Grand Rapids. The human resources director had good news. They had been given permission to hire one more person, just one… just Tom. The parent company had lifted the hiring freeze for Tom alone.

As Tom spoke on the phone to the director, a warm sense of God's presence flooded his being. He knew that there was nothing frozen in God's kingdom and that He could melt any obstacle.

Tom's new job started and his first check came the very week his severance ran out from his old job. God had provided. He had prayed to a God of details. He had asked for a frozen mountain to move into the lake and it had done so.

If a man is called a street-sweeper,
he should sweep streets even as Michelangelo
painted, or Beethoven composed music,
or Shakespeare wrote poetry.
He should sweep streets so well that all the hosts
of heaven and earth will pause to say,
Here lived a great street-sweeper
who did his job well.

GEORGE SMITH PATTON

His lord said to him,
'Well done, good and faithful servant;
you were faithful over a few things,
I will make you ruler over many things.
Enter into the joy of your lord.'

MATTHEW 25:21 NKJV

From One Foot-Six to Six Foot Five!

SPEAKING OF "good and faithful servants," Margaret is definitely one and she shares a wonderful story about one of her most awesome answers to prayer. It's a prayer story about her fifth and last baby.

When her baby boy was diagnosed with hyaline membrane (or respiratory distress syndrome) on the day of his birth, Margaret's doctor told her to summon her pastor to baptize the baby because he would not live through the night. Stricken with grief, Margaret poured out her heart before God in every way she knew how. Since she and her husband had not really planned a fifth child, believing they could only support four realistically and ever hope to put them through college, she reminded God that this baby was His idea. If this baby was indeed conceived because he was God's idea, then by all means he should live and be brought into the world, she reasoned.

When her son made it through the first night, Margaret continued her prayers until she was ultimately sent home and the baby remained in the hospital learning how to breathe without exhaustion. Margaret visited her newborn every day at the hospital and continued in her prayers for his total recovery. She never wavered in her belief in God's promises for the good of her son.

When Margaret went back to her own doctor for her post partum checkup, the doctor inquired as to what diagnosis her baby had been given. When she told her doctor the diagnosis, the doctor was dumbstruck. Margaret smiled and said that she called her son her "power of prayer baby." It was obvious to Margaret that her doctor did not believe the baby should have survived.

As we look at this miracle, we have to keep in mind that this event took place over thirty-five years ago, so techniques available to save such babies today weren't in place then. Prayer was indeed the power behind this healing.

Years later, when Margaret's now nearly six-foot-five son was on his way to college, she recalled some of the fears she and her husband had faced during her pregnancy. One concern was paying for another child to go to college on the salary of a school teacher. As she looked back at that fear, she gave God credit for His great sense of humor and His desire to provide. This son was her only child to go to college on a full scholarship. Like so many worries, this one never came to pass.

After he graduated from college, Margaret felt God was at work once again in her son's life when he revealed to her that he wasn't happy in his career choice. Her son said that he discovered he only really came to life when he was teaching a Bible study or leading a prayer group. This time, when Margaret's son wanted to go back to college again to become a pastor, she prayed again about his choice and whether she should support him financially. She felt God telling her to just step back and let Him take care of things. Margaret's once-struggling-to-breathe tiny baby grew into a dynamic pastor, who today gives breath to his own flock and life to his own four children.

When a believing person prays, great things happen.

JAMES 5:16 NCV

"What Can You Pray For?"

You can pray for **TRUTH**
Or new direction,
Pray for **LOVE**
Or deep affection,
Pray for **FRIENDS**
Or family too,
Pray for **OTHERS**
Or just for you,
Whatever you feel
Whatever is real…
Just start **TODAY**,
TAKE TIME TO PRAY!

KAREN MOORE

Prayer is a sincere, sensible, affectionate
pouring out of the soul to God, through Christ
in the strength and assistance of the Spirit,
for such things as God has promised.

JOHN BUNYAN

"Also, I TELL YOU
that if two of you on earth
agree about something
and PRAY FOR IT,
it will be done for you
by my Father in heaven.
This is true because if two or three people
come together in my name,
I AM THERE with them."

MATTHEW 18:20 NCV

Who Is Faithful, Lord?

MATTERS OF THE HEART can often put us to the test. They test our sense of self-worth, our sense of faith in the good things of life, our sense of reason, and the ability to understand the actions of others. Heartache, sadly enough, is a rather universal predicament. Many of us have been through those doors and what didn't kill us, made us stronger. Let's look at a broken hearted man who found God's peace on the verge of despair.

Most of us marry in good faith. We believe once we've chosen someone that we will spend our days and nights living in joy and in love for the rest of our lives. Sadly, it is often not the case. When Michael discovered that his wife was being unfaithful, he offered her an olive branch of forgiveness and worked harder at the marriage. The next time she was unfaithful, he found it a bit more difficult to be forgiving, but was determined to honor his commitment and once more worked with his wife to strengthen their bond.

His children were still young and Michael felt he was doing the right thing to keep the family together. One day though, he just couldn't do it any more. He discovered that his wife was now having an affair with his best friend. He found out when someone anonymously sent him a letter at work to share this information. He was devastated.

After receiving the letter, he wandered around the office feeling numb and hopeless. He looked out the window and considered just jumping off the building. After all, he had tried everything and had already been as forgiving as he knew how. He just didn't know what else to do.

As he stood pondering the possibility of that, he found himself praying. "Lord," he said, "if you're there, I need you." Within moments, he felt a breath of peace pass through him. It was an immediate and gentle response. For what seemed like the first time in his adult life, he knew that God was indeed there.

The next week at church, Michael decided at the last moment to attend a renewal service. In the group, he shared how lonely he often felt at church. A couple seated near him reminded him that God loved him at that very moment. Once again, Michael felt the peace and the realization of just how personal God can be. Michael was ready to take God to heart.

Though Michael may have felt that all of his efforts to be forgiving hadn't really worked, I'd like to think that they are part of the reason God showed him mercy as soon as he asked for it. Your prayers matter to God. You are precious to Him.

God said to Moses,

"I will show KINDNESS
to anyone to whom I want to show kindness,
and I will show MERCY
to anyone to whom I want to show mercy."
So GOD WILL CHOOSE the one
to whom he decides to show mercy;
his choice does not depend
on what people want or try to do.

ROMANS 9:15-16 NCV

Prayer is the soul's sincere desire,
Uttered or unexpressed;
The motion of a hidden fire
That trembles in the breast.

JAMES MONTGOMERY

Our biblical ancestors had their share of disappointments, betrayals, and heartaches. When we read the stories of Abraham and Sarah, or David and Bathsheba, or Ruth and Boaz, we realize that no matter how sophisticated we might believe we are in the world today, our hearts battle the same predicaments, the same brokenness, the same unquenchable love of generations before us. In some way, it's comforting. In some way, it makes us wonder why we haven't gotten better at building and sustaining relationships. It's safe to say that the same loving God rules the universe and watches over our hearts with the same compassion. Sometimes in relationships, more than any other place, we can get the definite feeling that we haven't got a prayer.

Waiting For Her Own Gadot

JANE'S HUSBAND LEFT HER when she was barely thirty, with two small children, no work experience, and no place to go. He said she didn't "fit" into his life. Fortunately, she had a loving sister who embraced her and helped her get back on her feet again. Within a week, she found a job and then in the years that followed, she prayed for a new partner.

She understood when he didn't show up through the first several years of her prayers because she had some baggage to unload. Around ten years later though, she started wondering if a new life partner would ever show up. She took that time to get to know herself, become more of the person she meant to be all along, raised her children, and kept a living relationship with the Lord.

Thirteen years later, her kids were nearly grown and the years had somehow evaporated into the mists of time. With no partner in sight, she finally gave up.

Shortly after giving up, she was invited by a friend to go to a dance. She didn't know anyone except the woman she went to the dance with, so she stayed on her own most of the time. God had bigger plans though and Don walked into her life. Her friend encouraged her to make the first move. Jane found that hard to do, but reluctantly asked Don if he'd like to dance and the love story began. Or so, she thought…

After five years of dating, they had not yet made plans to marry and Jane was getting to the end of her desire to be a date forever. She finally broke things off, hoping it would challenge Don into making a commitment. They separated for a year.

Finally, that Christmas, Don sent Jane a Christmas card and instead of being glad to receive it, she felt angry. She sent him a note and suggested that either he get into her life, or stay out of it, but she didn't want it both ways. Shortly after receiving her note, Don asked if Jane would consider having dinner with him so they could talk. She agreed. Two days later, he proposed.

They've been married now for a number of delightful years. They both give God the glory and are grateful for the many steadfast prayers that brought them together. Perhaps Don discovered the same thing that G. K. Chesterton experienced when he said, "the way to love anything is to realize that it might be lost."

Clearly the God of love did not want either of them to suffer loss. God is infinite love, unconditional love, and the standard of love. If we can even conceive a portion of that love He offers us and share that love with another, we are blessed.

Love is the fulfillment of all our works.

There is the goal;

that is why we run:

we run toward it, and once we reach it,

in it we shall find rest.

Augustine of Hippo

The Lord is righteous in all His ways,
Gracious in all His works.
The Lord is near to all who call upon Him,
To all who call upon Him in truth.
He will fulfill the desire of those who fear Him;
He also will hear their cry and save them.
The Lord preserves all who love Him,
But all the wicked He will destroy.

Psalm 145:17-20 NKJV

Doing God's Work!

PAM'S STORY takes on a more global community aspect and shows us how God can answer the prayers of two very different people who are worlds apart, and bring them together for His glory.

In 1988, Pam took a trip to England for the Dunstan Millennium—a celebration honoring St. Dunstan—and people from St. Dunstan Episcopal, Anglican, and Roman Catholic churches around the world were coming together to celebrate. On the second day of the gathering, Pam was visiting an old church and was looking at the beautiful stained glass windows and the inside pews. Noticing a side altar with a cross and fresh flowers, Pam moved in that direction to give herself more room. As she reached the altar, she felt that someone was right behind her and she turned to find a priest from Africa that she had noticed the day before in a gathering out in the street. He was one of only two black faces she had seen in the crowd.

The priest addressed Pam and said, "I have been watching and praying, and you are the one." A surprised Pam asked him to repeat what he said.

He told Pam and her husband that he was from a small village in South Africa called Maltino. He said that they had no altar clothes for their church and that he had been praying about this and that God sent him to Pam. The couple agreed that they would do all that they could to get some altar hangings for the St. Dunstan's church in Maltino.

When Pam and her husband returned to Houston, they checked with the Diocesan Altar Guild office and were told that they indeed had altar hangings that they could pick from for the priest's church. They were able to find some appropriate pieces for each of the church seasons. Though they didn't all match, they were in good shape.

When the priest received the hangings, he sent a beautiful letter to Pam thanking her for their gifts and generosity. He said they had just completed a new building and the altar hangings arrived in time for the celebration.

The joy of this blessing was two-fold. The priest prayed for direction and the right person to connect with about his need for altar clothes. Pam's prayer had been one that said, "God, help me to do Your work this day. Use me, guide me, and help me not to turn away." Two beautiful prayers, both answered, and both brought great blessings.

Communicating our questions, hopes,

and fears in prayer makes them—

even to ourselves—more open and clear;

and the stronger the ties that bind us to God,

the more likely we are to live, react, and behave

in harmony with exalted standards—

and with greater joy, peace, and happiness.

PRESIDENT JIMMY CARTER

All our words will be useless

unless they come from within.

Words that do not give the light of Christ

increase the darkness.

Today, more than ever, we need to pray

for the light to know the will of God,

for the love to accept the will of God,

for the way to do the will of God.

MOTHER TERESA

Parents and Children

IT'S HARD TO IMAGINE a more heartfelt prayer than the prayers of parents for their children. It's especially difficult when the children you've raised in faith and the teachings of prayer and Bible readings since the day they were born, make a choice as they reach adulthood to reject everything you thought they knew. That was the situation for Steve and Molly.

Steve's son and daughter had both accepted the Lord as young children and then stopped following God during their teen years. As parents, they did what they could to encourage their children to attend church, but realized after several efforts that pushing them did not seem to be the answer. They decided to stop pushing and start praying harder. They asked God to always keep His hand on their children, create positive relationships for them with Christian friends, and bring them back to Himself again of their own free will. They even threw into the prayer the notion that the children didn't have to do this to please them, not that they expected that response from their teenagers, but to please God. They continued to pray and enlisted friends to pray as well.

Fifteen years passed. Steve and Molly stopped addressing their concern over their children with friends and had chosen to pray about it on their own. They didn't realize at the time that some of their friends had continued to faithfully pray for their children all those fifteen years. Both kids were now fully grown, married, and beginning families of their own.

In September of 2000, Steve and Molly learned that their son had had a "chance" encounter with a former heavy metal rock band member at a local grocery store. The former band member was now playing at a local chapel and invited Steve's son and his wife to join them.

When they visited the church, the young couple discovered that their spiritual emptiness had been more painful than they had even realized. They created new relationships in this Christian community and felt fulfilled once more. They committed themselves to the Lord once again and became active members of the church. Two years later, they were both baptized, along with their young son.

As only God can do things, that same month, Steve's daughter called him to say that one of their friends had invited her and her husband to visit his church. This friend had invited them several times before and so they finally gave in and decided to visit. To their joy and surprise, they found a home in this large and friendly community of believers and became regular attendees.

Steve and Molly rejoiced at knowing that their children were indeed back in the fold. God had used two very different friends, each named Dave, to hold up His mirror to these beloved children and reflect His grace and blessing.

As parents, it's not always easy to accept the choices our children make. Sometimes we have to let them go and trust God to deliver on His promises in His own way and in His own time. We have to keep praying and know that He holds them in His hand. Steve and Molly learned great lessons in trust and the answers to their prayers were graciously delivered.

The fifteen years of heartfelt prayer may not seem like an overnight success, but in the big picture, we can graciously see God's timing.

Little drops of water,

　　　little grains of sand,

Make the mighty ocean

　　　and the beauteous land.

And the little moments,

　　　humble though they be,

Make the mighty ages of eternity.

Julia Carney

We might amend the prayer of St. Benedict as we pray for our children into something like this:

Father,

Give us WISDOM to perceive You,

INTELLECT to understand You,

DILIGENCE to seek You,

and PATIENCE to wait for You

as we pray for our children.

Grant us EYES to behold You,

HEARTS to meditate on You

and LIVES to proclaim You

in all that we do. Through the power

and Spirit of our Lord Jesus Christ,

we ask that You protect and preserve

our children in Your grace.

AMEN.

Sometimes a Prayer Takes on Wings

CAROL ATTENDED a spiritual reflections retreat in Montreat, North Carolina with her sister. They enjoyed four glorious days of prayer, meditation, Bible study and beautiful autumn scenery. After the intense study, powerful sense of community, and gifts of reflection, they were ready to get on home and share some of their incredible experiences.

As they headed for the airport and their scheduled flight, a new friend they had made at the retreat was right behind them. She was anxious to get home to her family as well and she hoped she'd be able to fly with them. When they checked in at the desk though, they were told that the flight was totally booked. The ticket agent offered to put Janice, their new friend, on stand by, but she told them there were already two people ahead of her so her chances were pretty slim.

The three women bowed their heads and prayed that a seat would open up. As the boarding process was underway, the name of the first standby person was called. He walked up to the ticket counter and eventually came back to his seat, which was right behind the women. They overheard him say to his companion, "I'm not going to take this flight because I want to travel with you."

The three women heaved a "Thank You, Jesus" sigh. Moments later when Janice's name was called, they were smiling and laughing as they all boarded the plane.

Prayer is far more than a flight of fancy.

Any concern too small
to be turned into a prayer
is too small
to be made into a burden.

CORRIE TEN BOOM

A Little Righteous Prayer

IN 1985, TINA FELT GOD leading her to open an Adult
Daycare Program. She started with one woman whom she
took shopping and on easy outings, then there were two, then
three. She enjoyed caring for these older citizens and spent
most of the days indoors in the small room provided at the
local senior center.

As an RN, she realized that some of these people had
medical problems beyond Alzheimer's disease and that there
was a very real possibility of a medical emergency. This was
long before cell phones and the nearest phone that Tina could
reach was down a long hallway and a flight of stairs.

She began to pray to God for the money to be able to put
a new phone system into the Daycare room. Tina's heart was
all about serving God's people and doing a work that she believed God meant for her to do. She realized how important it
was for her to keep her people safe and being able to respond
to a medical emergency was certainly part of that. She determined that she needed $500 for the new phone system and
began to pray specifically for the money.

She asked every group she could think of for help to get
the phone in the program room, but no one responded. While
she prayed for the phone, she also prayed that no emergency
would erupt in the meantime. Tina appreciated those in her

care and believed they still had gifts and talents to share with others. She wanted to keep them together to encourage their hearts and minds.

She continued to pray, going to Mass often and putting the problem before God. Finally, at one Mass, she told God that it didn't look like the money for the phone was going to come in and that perhaps it was not God's plan after all for her to do this. She decided God was telling her that the program should not go on. She said, "God, I will accept Your will and close the program before anyone has an emergency and I am not able to get to a phone in time." Feeling sad about the whole thing, Tina set about preparing the way to inform the board, and the families involved with the program, that she would have to close things down. Months of prayer had been to no avail.

The very day she was prepared to close the door, she found a note from a board member in her mailbox. The note instructed her to get the phone installed for the program, and was complete with a personal check for $500 to get the job done. Tina knew that God had answered. The program would go on.

Today, the program that Tina started to care for elderly seniors is still in place and has helped hundreds of older people and their families through very difficult times.

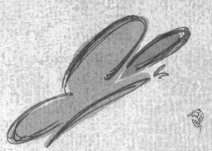

Inside the will of God,
there is no failure,
Outside the will of God,
there is no success.

BERNARD EDLINGER

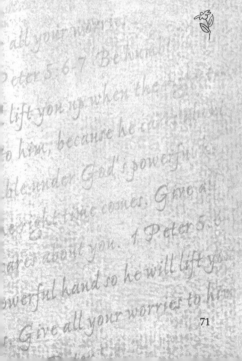

When It's Nothing
Short of a Miracle...

THE INCREDIBLE STORY that follows is about a faithful woman named Ruth and her tiny daughter, Sierra. Prayers for healing are born in any situation where we must truly surrender the outcome to God's loving hand.

It all started on a Sunday and what appeared to be a normal, busy day in April. Ruth and the children, Sierra aged five, and Jacob aged twelve, were happily planning a birthday celebration for the children's dad. Attending church that morning, they listened to a sermon on healing, and Ruth thanked God that her family was healthy and sound, both physically and emotionally. She thanked God for keeping her children safe.

After church, Ruth and her family ran some errands, and came home around five o'clock in the afternoon. Everyone was pretty tired, but the kids decided to go out in the back yard and jump on the family trampolines. They had two of them and the kids had jumped on them a million times.

About forty-five minutes into what seemed like a pretty ordinary event, Ruth's son, Jacob, ran into the house to say that Sierra had fallen and hit the ground pretty hard. Running outside, they found Sierra sitting somewhat dazed between the trampoline and the house. She was crying, but not hysterically.

Ruth asked her if she could stand up and she tried, but said it hurt to do so. She then asked Sierra if she could move her head and wiggle her toes. Ruth picked her child up and set her carefully on the family room sofa. Sierra had stopped crying by then, and checking for bruises on her tummy and potential fractured ribs, Ruth determined that she seemed to be okay.

Sierra was tired and wanted to sleep so Ruth tucked her in on the couch and watched her breathe. But just a half hour later, Sierra woke up crying and Ruth made another effort to find out where she might be hurting. At that point, Sierra vomited and they headed directly for the emergency room. As they sped to the ER, Ruth prayed for their safety in getting there and for Sierra to be all right.

By 9 p.m., they determined after ultrasounds, x-rays, and cat scans, that Sierra had ruptured her spleen. They admitted her to the ICU and put a tube in her stomach, gave her a plasma transfusion, and started her on morphine. Sierra, awake through the whole process was strong and brave and didn't even cry. They drew her blood every four hours to be sure that internal bleeding had subsided.

Because Sierra was in so much pain, she was only able to breathe in a very shallow way. This caused her left lung to shrink and the cavity around it to fill up with fluid. The only way to avoid needing to insert a drainage tube or a needle to suck out the fluid was to have Sierra begin to breathe normally.

By Monday morning, Ruth had all her friends, her church, her husband's co-workers and nearly anyone else she could find praying for her daughter to breathe in a normal fashion. Everybody was praying.

They were able to remove the tube to her stomach, but she wasn't able to eat or drink anything. They needed to give her oxygen to help expand her lung.

By Tuesday, the miracles started coming in. An x-ray taken in the early morning showed the lung to be amazingly better.

As Thursday came, Sierra was allowed a liquid diet, some jello and broth. They took out the IVs, leaving only one for saline and one to withdraw blood. They also took her off morphine.

By the Grace of God, as Friday came and went and Saturday appeared, she got better every minute. She was able to eat again and function on her own. Finally, as Sunday came again, she was allowed to go home.

As Ruth looked at the enormity of the situation and all that her little girl had gone through, she realized how many prayers had been answered. She knows that prayer kept Sierra out of surgery and from having the fluid around her lung extracted. Prayer kept her strong and brave and eventually brought the healing.

Reflecting on her own ordeal of eight hospital days, Ruth realized how many prayers had worked on her behalf as well. With an overwhelming sense of peace, Ruth knew that God walked beside her every minute, and that He, too, never slept, or ate, or removed His hand.

As the weeks have passed since that dreadful day, Sierra has gotten stronger and stronger. A recent cat scan revealed that her spleen now looked as though nothing had ever happened. Only God could put it all back together and give Sierra a second chance at life.

Lord,

For all those who don't yet know
Your mighty and powerful love,
please help them find You.
Pour out Your *mercy* on their hearts
and kindle the flame of *faith*
in a new and passionate way
into their spirits.
As they walk toward You, Lord
even a little bit,
run toward them as the Father did
in the story of the Prodigal son
and bring them back home again
to CELEBRATE in great joy.
May Your *light* shine on in their hearts
and minds forever.

AMEN.

Behold, children are a heritage from the Lord,
The fruit of the womb is a reward.

PSALM 127:3 NKJV

IT'S AN AWESOME THING to see the prayers for our children answered in such remarkable ways. Ruth's story is a beautiful reminder to take our eyes off the circumstances around us and keep them focused on the One who can help. It is the duty of faith to overcome fear at every turn. It's not always easy to see that though, especially through blinding snow, as the next story shows.

Angel in the Snow

MY SON WAS BRAND NEW to the world, and as my first baby, I was in protective mode as I prepared to take all six pounds of him to visit our families for Thanksgiving. I was convinced that he might not be a baby at all, but perhaps an angel in a very tiny form.

My husband and I lived on Long Island, and that Thanksgiving we drove to upstate New York for the holiday. The trip usually took a little more than four hours to complete. Baby Doug was not quite a month old when we wrapped him in blankets and headed for the Throgs Neck Bridge to get to our family home.

In those days, babies weren't required to be in infant seats, in fact, they probably didn't even have such things then, so I carried him in my arms for most of the trip. As his father drove our car up and down the hills that got us closer to our parents, it began to snow. The snow quickly became a driving, blinding white out and our car began to not take the hills very well. We started to get concerned that our car was having some mechanical problems, but there was nothing we could do out in the middle of a snowstorm on a very dark night. We were already well onto country roads that offered little in the form of helpful pull off spots.

Seeing that we were barely making it up one hill and down the other, I began to pray and I continued to pray all the way to my parent's door.

I was sure at one point that I literally felt the presence of an angel helping to get our crippled car over the snow-covered highways. I said, "Lord, please keep us safe and please don't let our car break down. My baby is so tiny and he would get cold so quickly if we were to have to sit very long on the side of the road to find help. Please protect us and surround us with your angels. Amen."

I remember to this day how quiet the night was and how much I yearned for the outside light that would be awaiting us at Mom and Dad's. We got through the storm and got home safely. The interesting thing was that once we got there, the car died in my parent's drive way and we had to have it towed the next day to a garage to be repaired. I knew the prayers were all that made it possible for us to enjoy that Thanksgiving as we intended and I'm still grateful to this day for God's help. He surely put His angels in the snow to help a little family and an ailing car.

> *For the eyes of the Lord are on the righteous,*
> *And His ears are open to their prayers…*
>
> 1 PETER 3:12 NKJV

Believing in God's Presence

SOMETIMES WE DON'T MOVE with the certainty that God is with us everyday. We don't rest in the knowledge that He goes ahead of us, knowing fully every step we'll take that day. Norman Vincent Peale spoke of the same idea in this way.

"One of the most powerful concepts, one which is a sure cure for lack of confidence, is the thought that God is with you and helping you. This is one of the simplest teachings in religion, namely, that Almighty God will be your companion, will stand by you, help you, and see you through. No other idea is so powerful in developing self-confidence as this simple belief when practiced. To practice it simply affirm "God is with me; God is helping me; God is guiding me." Spend several minutes each day visualizing his presence. Then practice believing that affirmation."

A Prayer of Meditation

Ponder on My truth,
Hold it in your mind,
Meditate on Me
Until we are aligned.
For I have much to teach
And much that I would share,
If you would seek Me out
And commune with Me in prayer.
Set apart some time
To come with Me and rest,
For when we're there together
Both of us are blessed.

KAREN MOORE

Healing Prayers

FOR ME, one of the toughest forms of prayer is around the subject of healing. An area of real spiritual growth for me, I was fascinated by the story of another crusade and a woman God put directly in my path so that her story could be shared. I know God meant for you to have this story because I met Sharon at a big conference of thousands of people. As I was walking in with a friend of mine, heading for a back row on the floor, a woman came up to us and asked if we would like to sit in the front row. We were surprised and pleased and followed her to the front row center of the arena. Sharon was sitting next to me. Here's her story.

God Heals Nurses and Doctors, Too

SHARON IS AN RN and developed arthritis in both of her hands…overnight. She went to bed one night and woke up the next day with crippling arthritis. At the time, Sharon was going through a lot of stress and felt bound by chains. She played the happy-go-lucky Christian woman on the outside, but was dying a slow mental and spiritual death on the inside.

The pain was so severe that any time her hands or fingers even touched or hit anything, she would scream out in pain. She could not open a jar at home, open her car door, or even do her job well. She could certainly not administer injections at the hospital or even write her own name. Bending her fingers in any way was shear agony.

Finding no medical relief, she started studying the Word of God. She was not merely reading it, she was starved for it, putting every word of it into her mind and spirit and preparing for the conference she planned to attend. She was ready for God to perform a miracle in her life and she intended to go to the crusade with the full expectation that it would happen.

By the time Sharon was sharing this story with me at the conference, she grasped my hand, hugged me, twirled her fingers through the air and praised God for the healing that had taken place that very day. Her fingers weren't the only things healed though, for as Sharon tells it, "the chains all fell away too." She is a new woman set free by the prayers and the hopes and the miracles of God.

Sharon is blessed with a new life, a new attitude, and has become a permanent believer in the power of prayer and richness of a life with God. She will never be in bondage again. As a woman in the healing profession, Sharon experienced first hand, or should we say, all the way down to her finger tips, the glory of God's answers.

Sharon's miracle came in part because she wisely prepared her heart and expectantly looked for the outcome. Charles Spurgeon said, "Neither prayer, nor praise, nor the hearing of the word will be profitable to those who have left their hearts behind them." Sharon's heart was ready to receive.

BOUND

Are you bound, beset by chains,
A prisoner of your own pains?
Are you trapped by strange deceit,
Believing you deserve defeat?
Does fear so like the spiders weave
Hold you taught, without reprieve?
Alas, my friend, you've been betrayed,
Those chains are only paper made.
That trap is just a cunning lie
For you are free enough to fly.
That web you're able to unfold
For at God's word, it cannot hold.
The prisons we so often find
Are simply matters of the mind.
Trust in Him to show the way,
He'll help you break those chains today.

KAREN MOORE

God does not delay our prayers

because He has no mind to give;

but that, by enlarging our desires,

He may give us the more largely.

ANSELM OF CANTERBURY

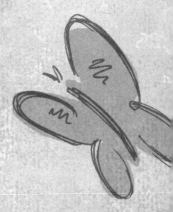

Faith In the Trial of Breast Cancer

WE ALL HAVE LITTLE PRAYERS and big prayers. Or do we? Perhaps every prayer is BIG because every prayer is a desire of the heart, and aligning our hearts with God's will and purpose is the key to all of it. Considering health issues though, probably there are no bigger prayers than the ones of a woman who has discovered a lump in her breast. Let's look at Sue's story and see the power of God at work.

SUE HAS BEEN a growing and practicing and faithful Christian all her life. As a nurse, she has the spirit of an angel and the heart of grace. She's attended to the needs of others both physically and spiritually most of her adult life.

In 1998, Sue was diagnosed with invasive breast cancer. As a believer, she understood that she could face this fact with fear and turn away from God, or she could focus on Him and bathe in His presence and watch His mighty hand at work. Easier said than done!

She chose to resist fear as much as possible and lean with her whole heart and mind and soul on the strength that only God could give her. Sue found God's strength through the love and faithfulness that He showered her with. He showed her His love through her husband, her children, and her many praying friends. She embraced the daily visits of friends through hugs, phone calls, cards and letters. Sue physically felt the hand of God on her shoulder and she didn't let go of Him when she faced surgery.

The night before she went into surgery, she prayed more and she awoke with the strength to go into the halls of the Cancer Foundation. She relied on the Scripture from 2 Corinthians 1:3-4 which says, "Praise be to the God and Father of our Lord Jesus Christ. God is the Father who is full of mercy and all comfort. He comforts us every time we have trouble, so when others have trouble, we can comfort them with the same comfort God gives us" (NCV). Through the challenges before her, Sue started to perceive the world more fully through the eyes of the Holy Spirit. She saw the beauty of her own surroundings, the flowers, trees, and sunsets, as if for the first time.

She did not have to beg for peace. It came over her in abundance. Even in the rockiest times, Sue clung to the side of the Savior. As she and her husband awaited decisions about treatment or results of scans, they waited in the presence of God's strength and courage. Sue never experienced nausea from chemotherapy, a lack of sleep, depression or an inability to eat. She felt that God was in complete control of the situation and she rested in His care.

During the time of her treatment, Sue spent hours in prayer and meditation and absorbed the Word. She was awed by the numerous accounts in the Bible that offered encouragement and blessing. She knew people were praying for her in her family, in other cities, and other states and countries. She felt totally immersed in their prayers. She felt safe.

Today she is cancer free and delights in the glory of His love and faithfulness. One of the outcomes of Sue's experience with cancer is that she learned how important it really is for us to pray for one another. She says, "It is a wonderful privilege to take another person to Jesus' feet for healing." Sue believes that God healed her through His amazing grace, through her physicians, and the medications engineered through medical science. She experienced God's personal power every day of her illness.

Sue is thankful that she has always had a personal relationship with God, but she is even more grateful that He prepared her a long time ago to be able to get through this difficult trial.

*"I say this because I know
what I am planning for you," says the Lord.
"I have good plans for you,
not plans to hurt you.
I will give you hope and a good future.
Then you will call my name.
You will come to me and pray to me,
and I will listen to you.*

JEREMIAH 29:11-12 NCV

*The Lord himself will go before you.
He will be with you;
he will not leave you or forget you.
Don't be afraid and don't worry.*

DEUTERONOMY 31:8 NCV

*You, Lord, give true peace to those
who depend on you, because they trust you.
So, trust the Lord always,
because he is our Rock forever.*

Isaiah 26:3-4 NCV

> The artist is nothing without the gift,
> but the gift is nothing without work.
>
> EMILE ZOLA

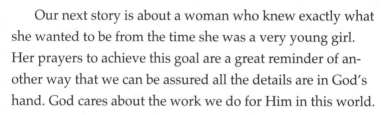

Our next story is about a woman who knew exactly what she wanted to be from the time she was a very young girl. Her prayers to achieve this goal are a great reminder of another way that we can be assured all the details are in God's hand. God cares about the work we do for Him in this world.

Margie's Dream Job

AS A LITTLE GIRL, not much older than five or six, Margie loved to go to a Hallmark store with her mother and just look at all the greeting cards on the rack. She loved the feel of the cards and the different looks of cards and knew that someday, she would be a person who worked for Hallmark. In those days, the inexpensive cards could be bought for a nickel, and Margie would gladly hand over her hard earned nickels to take home her prized cards.

During her high school years, her family moved to Kansas City, which is where the headquarters of Hallmark

Cards resides. Margie and her family took a tour of the facility and she set about the task of trying to determine what it would take to get in to the company.

While she was in college, she wrote to Hallmark to find out what she would need to do in order to apply for a job there. She was preparing to get a teaching degree. Through her four college years, she prayed continually that God would show her how to get the door open at Hallmark and to help her discover her true calling. She wasn't sure if she should be a teacher or get an art degree.

She graduated with a degree in English, but decided she really needed to keep going in school and also get an art degree as well. Her eye was on the goal and God's eye was on her dream. At the point of just finishing her art degree, a team of Hallmark recruiters visited the college Margie was attending and she went to the sessions with the recruiters and showed them her portfolio. They only had two slots open for upcoming jobs and happily, one of them went to Margie.

Margie was overjoyed and astounded at the grace of God in putting all the pieces together for her dream to come true. She had prayed for eight years for the fulfillment of this plan for her life.

As it turned out, she loved her job at Hallmark and worked there for several years. Since Kansas City was far from her family and friends however, she began to feel a need to be closer to them. Since she especially loved working on inspirational greeting card lines, she found a position in another greeting card company much closer to her family home and became the creative director of their inspirational programs. Again, she could see God's hand clearly at work in her life.

During the process of following God's lead, Margie was impressed often with the idea that God was speaking directly to her. In His way, He kept saying "just walk through it."

In other words, your prayers are being answered now, so just walk through the door of this opportunity knowing that you are indeed answering your calling.

There is one Lord, one faith, and one baptism.
There is one God and Father of everything.
He rules everything and is everywhere
and is in everything.
Christ gave each one of us the special gift of grace,
showing how generous he is.

EPHESIANS 4:5-7 NCV

Lord,

Help us to always seek

Your highest calling

and to pursue that calling

with the *passion*

You have ignited in our spirits

so that our GIFTS

may be shared

with one another

for the sake of Your kingdom.

AMEN.

Finding a New Path

BECAUSE OUR WORK PAYS our way in the world and also sustains our spirit, it's important to know that we're doing the work God intends for us to do. It's not uncommon today for a person to not just change jobs, but to literally change careers several times. Career changes of that sort take some risk and some pretty strong assurance that God is indeed leading the way. The next story illustrates just what God can do when we're ready to work with Him as we open the door to a new career.

Janice was in a new phase of life. She had been married, divorced, widowed, and married again. She had raised children, graduated from college, and enjoyed a career in the pharmaceutical industry on the sales side. Her company created cardiovascular and diabetes products and she had many opportunities to become very knowledgeable in those areas and related areas as well. She took formal training any time it was offered and learned a lot by going on lectures at teaching hospitals. Janice liked to do her homework and always felt that it was a key to understanding God's direction for her life.

But at the age of 49, she found herself miserably over-weight and physically unfit. She knew it was time to change her super mom, super wife and super employee status and start taking better care of herself. Janice started going to her local YWCA to work out, take classes, and do some weight lifting. She also decided to change her menu and start eating foods that were better for her body.

One of her favorite activities at the Y was taking a step aerobics class. Janice became fascinated by the instructors' abilities to cue the next moves and create patterns for the workouts. Since she found the instructors to be very approachable, she felt encouraged to ask if she could learn how to cue. One instructor, in particular, spent time with Janice and encouraged her to go through the formal certification process to be an aerobics instructor. Janice decided it would be a good thing for her to do, so at 52, she became certified and was able to teach a number of regular classes at the Y.

Janice took other classes as well and kept attending work-shops on fitness related topics. She felt better than she had in years and enjoyed her students. Janice began to consider retirement from her regular job and wondered what it would take for her to have a regular job in the Women's Fitness Center. She felt especially drawn to women who felt as she had, that they were too stressed, too busy, or too selfless to take charge of a corner of their own lives. Janice decided to continue the classes for herself that would allow her to become a certified personal trainer for these women. She knew she still had homework to do.

Janice lost her husband that year and had to believe more than ever that she was to leave her old career behind and follow her heart toward this new position. She decided to maintain her course to retire on her intended date and actively seek the right position in a women's gym. But not just any gym would do! Janice didn't want to be part of one of those gyms that was about making money first and about their clients second. She began to realize that it might not be as easy as she hoped for this to all come together. "God," Janice prayed, "we've been through so much this year, is this too much to ask that the right position at a women's fitness center might open up?"

That spring, while Janice was working at her local Y, the membership director took her aside to get her input about an idea the Board of Directors was considering. Apparently, some space that was close to the existing Y was soon to become available and the Board was considering renting the space to offer a Women's Health and Wellness Center. Janice was not only being asked her opinion, but whether she would enjoy working in a facility like this if they were to move forward with it. Janice was awestruck. The God of details was obviously well ahead of her and working on this project.

Since Janice had already planned to leave her other career by September, the October opening of the new facility was perfect for her. She expressed her heart that she believed the center would be very well received and that she would love to work there on a part time basis. She began to send thank you prayers up to God on the spot.

It all came about in a perfect way. The Women's Center functions today as a place where the mind, body, and spirit are nurtured. Janice treasures her work there and her clients. She did become a personal trainer and God directed her steps to an awareness of a vital need for women. Janice will soon do personal training with women who have bone loss and women who want to sensibly lose weight. She's also well aware of the personal training she received from God as He guided her steps to this new career path, answering a great need for women, and a very heartfelt prayer for herself.

All growth depends upon activity.
There is no development physically or intellectually
without effort, and effort means work.
Work is not a curse; it is the prerogative
of intelligence, the only means to adulthood,
the means and the measure of civilization.

CALVIN COOLIDGE

We are all weak, finite, simple human beings,
standing in the need of prayer.
None need it so much as those who think
they are strong, those who know it not,
but are deluded by self-sufficiency.

HAROLD C. PHILLIPS

For by grace you have been saved
through faith,
and that not of yourselves;
it is the gift of God, not of works,
lest anyone should boast.
For we are His workmanship,
created in Christ Jesus for good works,
which God prepared beforehand
that we should walk in them.

EPHESIANS 2:8-10 NKJV

The Leprosy of Life

WHEN SALLY'S SEVEN-YEAR-OLD SON was invited to Sunday School by a neighbor, she was less than thrilled. Divorced for several years and living with her boyfriend, she had no real knowledge of salvation or "churchy" things and thought the worldly side of life was all there really was. Since she didn't know her neighbor well, she figured she would take her son to the church herself. They would probably both be bored before the second song, so Sally didn't think this event would be very remarkable.

Fortunately, God had already gone to the service ahead of Sally. She walked into the church and immediately felt that something was different. The music and the singing made her feel comfortable. As she looked around the pews, her attention was drawn to a woman who was singing her heart out to the Lord. Sally couldn't figure out why she couldn't take her eyes off the woman until it hit her that she could see something in that woman's face, she'd never really seen in her own. That woman was at peace.

Sally didn't know what that would feel like since she'd never had such an experience in her life. Sally found herself fighting some irresistible emotion and tried desperately to remind herself why she didn't believe in God. After all, He had let her down numerous times already.

As the Pastor delivered the morning sermon, Sally was awed by his ability to read her mind. He seemed to address every misgiving she was playing over in the recesses of her heart and soul. She wondered if the neighbor could have tipped him off somehow. As she left the church that day, Sally was glad her son had enjoyed his experience because it gave her an excuse to tell him that maybe they'd go back and try it again.

Sally returned to the church for several weeks and found people enjoying things that she hadn't known in her life, things like peace, joy, and love. Since most of her life had been given over to the ways of the world, Sally felt pretty sure that this door was probably closed. After all, how could God forgive someone like her?

Someone gave her a Bible and one afternoon, Sally decided to see if she could try to say a little prayer. Not being quite sure how one went about the business of praying, Sally asked God if He was able to forgive her, and would He show her a verse in the Bible that might help her understand how that was possible. She opened at random to Luke 5:12, but didn't understand anything about the reading. She closed the book, not sure if anything had happened.

About a week later, Sally returned to the church and discovered an old friend whom she hadn't seen for a number of years. They talked a bit after church, and her friend invited

Sally to call her if she ever had any questions about her recent attempts at finding her faith.

That night, Sally prayed that God would reveal Himself to her in a dream and let her know that He was really real. She dreamed that the friend she met in church told her to read Luke 5:12. Sally woke herself in the middle of the night and wrote the dream down.

When she read her note in the morning and opened the Bible to the Scripture, there was the same verse she hadn't understood before. She called her friend from church and asked her if she could explain the verse and the dream. Her friend shared with her that she had prayed for Sally a good deal of the night. Sally was amazed. She couldn't imagine anyone doing such a thing for her.

Her friend explained the Bible passage and helped Sally understand that leprosy was an outward sign of inward sin and that the leper in the story was asking Jesus for forgiveness. Jesus said yes to the leper.

As her friend explained the verse, Sally looked down at her own hands. They were covered with scars and open, painful wounds caused by a lifetime of terrible eczema. At that moment, Sally realized God was real and that He was telling her that He would indeed forgive her if she would but come to Him and ask.

The next Wednesday night, Sally went to the church and listened to a powerful story by a man who once belonged to the Hell's Angels. After the speaker finished, the path of salvation was explained to everyone and an altar call was given. Sally didn't walk, she ran to the altar. She invited the living Son of God into her heart and into her life and into her sorrow and He met her there.

For the first time in many years, Sally discovered the power of prayer, the blessing of peace and the healing of the Holy Spirit, for her eczema disappeared as well. Sally began a new passion for the Living Lord and for life. She was redeemed, blessed, and changed by the power of prayer and the gift of God.

*When Jesus was in one of the towns, there was a man
covered with a skin disease. When he saw Jesus,
he bowed before him and begged him,
"Lord, you can heal me if you will." Jesus reached out
his hand and touched the man and said, "I will.
Be healed!" Immediately the disease disappeared.*

Luke 5:12–13 NCV

My Brother's Keeper

SOMETIMES WHAT SEEMS like reality to us, isn't really the case when we're in the care and keeping of God. The next story is a reminder that sometimes we have to trust the Lord beyond what seems like common sense.

In the early 80s, Mark was a field sales manager in Kentucky. Things went well in his initial business and he and his new wife were pleased that they could put some bonus money into the bank and save for a house.

Just a couple months into the New Year though, Mark's company decided to downsize and suddenly he and the whole field sales division found themselves without jobs. Unemployment and interest rates were both high then, as the economy was unstable.

As a young man with limited work experience, Mark found it difficult to find a new job. His wife was working an hourly position and they were able to live off the money from the previous year's bonus, but things were tight. Several months passed and by summer, Mark thought it best to take a job in construction to help their situation. He didn't want their nest egg to dwindle down too far.

As it turned out, the summer was difficult for someone else in Mark's family as well…his brother. His brother had been scammed on an international business deal and lost everything he had. Unfortunately, those he had invited into what he believed to be a good deal, wanted to press criminal charges against him unless they got their money back. Of course, Mark's brother no longer had any money to give them and so it was a bad situation all the way around.

As Mark and his wife discussed the situation, they weren't sure how to help. Without steady work, it was diffi- cult to consider giving Mark's brother what savings they had managed to hold on to. However, they spent time in prayer and asked God what they should do. When the prayers were finished, they felt quite clearly directed to give Mark's brother the money they had saved. Even though they wondered what God would do to help them make ends meet as well, they believed God had a plan and remained at peace about their choice.

God did not make them wait long. Within fifteen minutes of their heart-felt decision, Mark got a phone call. It was from an executive of a company where he had submitted a resume some five months earlier. The caller apologized for disturbing Mark so late at night, but wondered if they could talk a bit about a job opening that seemed like a perfect fit. He asked Mark to come in the following week for an interview. Mark had never interviewed with so much confidence. God was providing in a perfect way. Two weeks later he and his wife started a new life in North Carolina. It was the perfect job at the perfect time.

Mark learned what it means to be your "brother's keeper." He also learned that reasoning and logic and all those things we depend on, are not necessarily the final answer in determining the best course for our lives or the steps that we should take. Mark learned to trust God's Spirit and God's plan for his life. He learned that God is personal and that He truly cares about the details we face.

Therefore humble yourselves
under the mighty hand of God,
that He may exalt you in due time,
casting all your care upon Him,
for He cares for you.

1 PETER 5:7 NKJV

Prayer Is Simple

Prayer is so simple;

It is like quietly opening a door

and slipping into the very presence of God.

There in the stillness

To listen to His voice,

Perhaps to petition,

Or only to listen.

It matters not, just to be there,

in His presence…

In prayer.

You Can Go Home Again

BILL HAD MOVED out of Shreveport, Louisiana and he was bound and determined that he'd never go back. He graduated from college, married the woman of his dreams and headed to a promising job in Houston, Texas in international banking. His wife served as an accountant to a multinational oil company and they were feeling like they had the world by the tail. They bought a home, started a family, had lots of friends and attended a church full of people like them. It was a wonderful life!

Without any warning, life changed abruptly. Bill's father died in a tragic car accident and left his family devastated. He was the rock, the stability, the one everyone looked to for encouragement and advice. Bill's mother needed a great deal of support to help her through her fears of loneliness and depression. His brother was just starting college and struggled to maintain focus and motivation. Needless to say, their world had been shaken.

As Bill faced his own grief issues, he realized that he was no longer content with his career path at work. He pursued what he hoped were better opportunities, only to find the door shutting in his face.

For the first time in years, Bill began to entertain the idea of moving back to Shreveport. He thought he had the right motivation. After all, his mother needed more support, it was a good place to raise his family and he still had lots of friends there. He and his wife decided to make the move.

In no time at all, they began to doubt the wisdom of their choice. They had started out the move by living with Bill's mother. He had taken a job at nearly half of his former salary. Finally, they moved out of his mother's house on less than pleasant terms and Bill started looking for a new job. They missed their home in Houston, their old friends, and the income they had enjoyed. Bill felt totally at a loss and wondered what God was doing. The weaker he became, the louder God talked.

It finally dawned on Bill that maybe he was carrying a lot of pride about his abilities to provide and about his independence. Maybe God was trying to get him to recognize that Bill was not actually the one in control...God was. Turning humbly to the Lord, Bill confessed his pride and the transformation began.

Looking back, Bill can clearly see God's design for his life. Bill doesn't even take credit for having the wisdom to return to Shreveport. He can see that God had intentions for Bill and that it was His purpose to see that they were fulfilled. Bill knows that he first needed to strengthen his personal relationship with His Father in Heaven. He had to understand what it meant for him to become a truly beloved son of God.

Bill also needed to restore his relationship with his biological father, who had left the family when Bill was just a young boy. Through the power of forgiveness and God's grace, Bill and his father began to restore and heal the relationship they had lost so long ago.

Beyond this marvelous healing of relationships, Bill received a healing of his own, in terms of spiritual growth. Though Bill has not totally found his new path, he knows he is there for a valuable life lesson. He needed some time apart from his own success so that he could hear the Holy Spirit as He tried to direct the new journey for Bill and his young family. As Bill says, he isn't walking a perfect walk yet. He stumbles, he falls, and he gets up again and starts over because one day he'll find God's promised land.

For any of us that have walked through the wilderness and thought we'd be better off going back to Egypt, Bill's story is a reminder and a blessing. We're all in the business to learn to be God's children in all the best ways and walking with Him every step of the way gives us greater strength and joy, than walking apart from Him ever could. Though our journeys are sometimes desolate and sometimes fearful, we know we're not walking there alone. The One who is totally in control is right by our side, holding us securely in His hand.

The Turning Point

If we could make a lifetime map
To show us where we've been,
With little markers for the things we know,
We'd probably be surprised
At all the twists and turns
That took us off the path
We thought we'd go.
And yet, we'd see some special signs,
Some stops along the way
That kept us safely on the road
We're following today.
And sometimes, we would mark the place
Where we hit a rocky road
And had to make decisions
To help lighten up our load,
And that would be a turning point,
A place where we stood still
And bowed to hear our Father's voice
And listen to His will.
For all along the roadway,
He paused to help us learn
That there's only one Mapmaker
And He's there at every turn.

KAREN MOORE

112

Through the Darkness of Depression

BETH DIDN'T LEAVE HOME for four and a half years! Most of the time, she'd sit in the corner of her closet, or hide under the bed. She was sure if she went out, she'd be killed, and her panic attacks consistently rendered her powerless. That's what life was like for Beth.

The only trips into the outside world that she could make during that time were to the doctor. Even those had to be carefully planned with the help of medication and psychologists. Nothing seemed to make her condition any better.

As the mother of four boys, one with down syndrome, and the wife of a good man, Beth and her family hoped and prayed she'd be healed.

Finally, Beth heard about a pastor who seemed to be having phenomenal results with his healing ministry. She heard about people who were experiencing miracles simply by attending one of his services. Beth wasn't sure she could go to a church service without a serious panic attack, but she began to pray for the miracle of being able to attend a service to receive her own healing.

After some time and a lot of encouragement, she ventured out of the house and went to the healing service of Pastor Steve Hill in Brownsville, Texas. Somehow, to her joy she got through the service and was able to attend each week for the next month. At the end of that month, she was healed.

Beth took small steps to freedom as her depression lifted. She went to the grocery store. Those of us who complain about going to the grocery store might not see the joy she had in being able to pick out her own vegetables again, but it was exciting to her. From there she listened to family radio with her husband and made attempts to connect with him and come back into his life. Why he hadn't left her already, Beth wasn't sure, but she was glad he was still there.

She worked her way up to the day when she could go out of the house without her husband or anyone for that matter. After long years of darkness, she emerged into the light with the joy of someone seeing the world for the very first time.

Beth's depression has been gone for two years now. She sings in the choir, works part time as a receptionist at the church and is grateful for the miracle of the answered prayer she received.

Beth's story is a reminder that God is the same yesterday, today, and forever. The miracles of long ago are still happening today. The blind receive sight, the depressed receive light, the hungry are fed, prayers are said, God is still there... everywhere!

Our desire to pray is the result
of God's call to prayer.
He has something to say.
Our responsibility is to listen
to what He wants to give us
in response to our problems and potentials.
He will make it clear.

JOHN OGILVIE

*The Lord is my rock and my fortress
and my deliverer; My God, my strength,
in whom I will trust;
My shield and the horn of my salvation,
my stronghold. I will call upon the Lord,
who is worthy to be praised;
So shall I be saved from my enemies.*

PSALM 18:2-3 NKJV

The Tulip and The Oak

SOMETIMES WE NEED a little help remembering that it isn't to our best advantage to go around comparing ourselves to everyone else. If we do that too much, we can find ourselves wondering if we're doing anything worthwhile or if we've missed the bull's eye completely. Those are times when we need to check in with God through prayer and get a little Fatherly advice and direction. Mark learned this lesson and wanted to share it with you.

IT'S NOT ALWAYS EASY to recognize when the heavy spirit of depression starts to overlay our lives and sometimes it blankets our spirits before we even know what happened. During one particular season, Mark found himself in just that place, when things in his life refused to go well. Feeling somewhat like he didn't have a prayer and the world was falling apart, Mark decided to go outside for a run. Running usually helped clear his head and made him feel better.

As he headed down the gravel road, he started praying to God about his situation. His answer came in the form of a parable about a tulip and an oak tree. It went something like this:

It's not easy being a tulip out here on this windy plain. Every year, I come back in the spring and I try really hard to do what I'm supposed to do. After a long winter's sleep, it's not all that easy to sprout new leaves and drink in another new season. The struggles never let up. Year after year, I deal with the same issues of heat, and wind, and hail, and I get so thirsty I could just choke to death. Inside, I secretly wish I was that big oak tree over there.

The oak tree is strong and pumps water through its system long after mine is gone. Even when I get to bloom, the winds come along and snap all my pretty petals away before anyone even notices I'm there. I feel so fragile and insignificant. I just wish I was an oak tree. Then I would be really special.

The next year, I come back again. I'm still a tulip. But for some reason, it was a good year for me. The heat didn't scorch my blooms, and I drank in the rain like fine nectar, and I dodged all the hail as I danced in the winds. It was great! When I was at the peak of my beauty, a wonderful thing happened. I was noticed by a little girl. She stooped down and looked at me and said how beautiful I was and that she thought I was a magnificent treasure. In fact, I was so beautiful that she wanted to take me home to her mother as a gift.

Her mother instantly recognized me as a very special tulip indeed. She thanked her daughter for her great love and thoughtfulness to bring her such a gift. I realized right then and there that God really did have a purpose just for me. I was a tulip and He created me and He wanted me to be the most beautiful tulip I could be and that would be my gift to the world. I discovered that I didn't have to be an oak tree after all.

What Mark learned on his run that day lifted his spirits. He experienced the joy of believing that even when times are hard, even when it looks like others are doing better, that God has a perfect plan just for him. God sees Mark's journey and knows what he's here for and He will perfect the path to take Mark where he needs to be. Mark doesn't need to compare himself to other people. He needs to be who he is and let God's light shine through him.

Four Steps to Prayer

STEP ONE: Call out to your Father in Heaven

STEP TWO: Thank God for His grace and mercy and invite Him to be with you as you pray

STEP THREE: Put your heartfelt requests and praises before Him

STEP FOUR: Pray in Jesus' name for His will to be done

And always rest in His love, believing your prayers are answered!

Some Prayers for Your Heart

For those who have used up every prayer you know and need a little help to get you back on track again, I include these prayers for your spirit, your soul, and for the good of your life.

May the Lord bless you with all good and keep you from all evil; may He give light to your heart with loving wisdom, and be gracious to you with eternal knowledge; may He lift up His loving countenance upon you for eternal peace.

DEAD SEA SCROLLS

Grant that I may not pray alone with the mouth; help me that I may pray from the depths of my heart.

MARTIN LUTHER

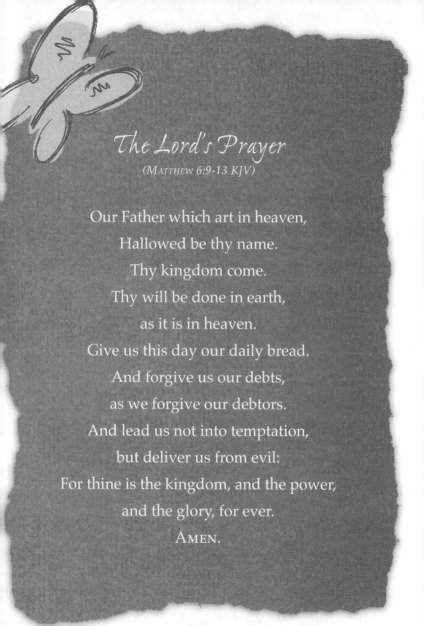

The Lord's Prayer
(MATTHEW 6:9-13 KJV)

Our Father which art in heaven,
Hallowed be thy name.
Thy kingdom come.
Thy will be done in earth,
as it is in heaven.
Give us this day our daily bread.
And forgive us our debts,
as we forgive our debtors.
And lead us not into temptation,
but deliver us from evil:
For thine is the kingdom, and the power,
and the glory, for ever.
AMEN.

The Breastplate of St. Patrick

I rise today with the power of God to guide me,
The might of God to uphold me,
The wisdom of God to teach me,
The eye of God to watch over me,
The ear of God to hear me,
The word of God to give me speech,
The hand of God to protect me,
The path of God to lie before me,
The shield of God to shelter me,
The host of God to defend me against the snares
Of the devil and the temptations of the world,
Against every man who meditates injury to me,
Whether far or near.

Help me, *O Lord,*
To know what I should know
and love what I should love.
Help me to PRAISE what delights You most
and value what is precious in Your sight.
Grant that I would hate what offends You.
Help me not to judge others blindly
or out of ignorance.
Help me only to discern
a TRUE judgment
between the spiritual
and visible
and the things that are
according to YOUR WILL.
AMEN.

(ADAPTED FROM THOMAS Á KEMPIS)

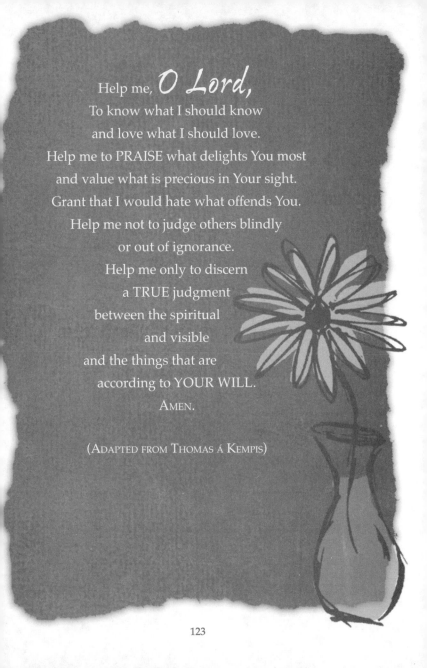

The Lord Is My Shepherd

(PSALM 23 NKJV)

The Lord is my shepherd;
I shall not want.
He makes me to lie down in green pastures;
He leads me beside the still waters.
He restores my soul;
He leads me in the paths of righteousness
For His name's sake.
Yea, though I walk through the valley
of the shadow of death,
I will fear no evil; For You are with me;
Your rod and Your staff, they comfort me.
You prepare a table before me in the presence
of my enemies;
You anoint my head with oil; My cup runs over.
Surely goodness and mercy shall follow me
All the days of my life;
And I will dwell in the house of the Lord Forever.

Book of Hours, 1514

God be in my head,
And in my understandings;
God be in my eyes,
And in my looking;
God be in my mouth,
And in my speaking;
God be in my heart,
And in my thinking;
God be in my end,
And in my departing.

From Numbers 6:24-26 NKJV

"May the Lord bless you and keep you.
May the Lord show you his kindness
and have mercy on you.
May the Lord watch over you
and give you peace."

notes

prayers